Persuade with Power: Mastering the Psychology of Influence

Unlock Proven Principles to Elevate Your Marketing, Sales, and Communication Strategies

By

Nicola I. Kattan

BOOK BOUND PRESS

https://web.facebook.com/BookboundPress/

3

Preface

In a world where attention spans are fleeting and competition for influence is fierce, the ability to persuade has never been more valuable. Whether you are presenting a business proposal, marketing a product, or simply communicating an idea, the power to influence others is an essential skill that can shape outcomes and create opportunities. Yet, influence is not merely a tool for selling—it is an art and science that extends into every facet of human interaction.

Persuade with Power: Mastering the Psychology of Influence is your comprehensive guide to unlocking this vital skill. This book is not just a collection of strategies; it is a journey into the psychology that drives human behavior and decision-making. By understanding the underlying principles of influence, you will gain the ability to inspire action, foster trust, and connect with others on a profound level.

The principles outlined in these pages are grounded in research from psychology, behavioral economics, and communication studies, yet they are presented in a way that is both practical and accessible. Each chapter builds upon the last, taking you step by step through the nuances of persuasion. From crafting compelling narratives to leveraging social proof, from understanding cognitive biases to mastering nonverbal communication, this book equips you with the tools to elevate your personal and professional interactions.

As you embark on this exploration, you will discover that influence is not about manipulation or coercion. It is about authenticity, empathy, and the ability to understand and address the needs and desires of your audience. When done effectively, persuasion becomes a powerful force for good—a way to inspire change, build relationships, and create win-win outcomes.

Each chapter of this book is designed to stand alone as a valuable resource while contributing to a larger framework of influence mastery. Whether you are a seasoned professional looking to refine your skills or a newcomer eager to learn the foundations, this book offers insights and techniques that can be applied immediately.

In Chapter 1, you will explore the psychology of influence and the foundational role of trust. Subsequent chapters will guide you through storytelling, rapport building, and the strategic use of language. Along the way, you will learn how to harness emotional appeals, overcome objections, and negotiate effectively. The concluding chapters focus on measuring success and adapting your strategies to achieve lasting impact.

The goal of **Persuade with Power** is not just to inform but to empower. By mastering the art of persuasion, you will not only achieve your objectives but also enrich your interactions with others. The principles in this book are timeless, yet they are more relevant than ever in today's interconnected and dynamic world.

As you turn the page, I encourage you to approach this book with curiosity and a commitment to growth. The skills you gain here have the potential to transform how you communicate, lead, and connect. Influence is not reserved for the naturally charismatic or the seasoned marketer—it is a skill anyone can develop with practice and intention.

Welcome to the journey of mastering the psychology of influence. Let this book be your guide to unlocking the power within you to persuade, inspire, and achieve greatness in all that you do.

Nicola I. Kattan								November 2024

Introduction

In a world overflowing with info, grabbing attention is tougher than ever. Whether you're selling something, leading a team, or just trying to change someone's mind, knowing how to influence is crucial. It's not just about slick tricks; it's about diving into how people think and connecting with them.

Picture this: you're in front of a crowd, each person a mix of hopes, fears, and dreams. What if you could untangle their thoughts and tell a story that hits home so hard they can't help but act? Persuasion isn't just for the naturally charming; it's a skill anyone can hone. Get a grip on the basics of influence, and you can level up your marketing, sales, and personal chats like never before.

Trust is the heartbeat of persuasion. It's
delicate but super powerful. When you're
interacting with others, knowing what they want
and need is key. You can't just throw out a
message; you've gotta tell a story that pulls at
their heartstrings and aligns with their dreams.
Storytelling's been around forever, and when
done right, it builds a bridge between you and
your audience, sparking a connection that drives
them to act.

Building rapport? That's essential. Use
techniques that create real connections. When
you make people feel seen and heard, they're
way more likely to buy into what you're saying.
Active listening, mirroring, and matching aren't
just tricks—they're the bedrock of solid
relationships.

Words are your secret weapon. The right
words can spark inspiration and get people
moving. Pay attention to tone and delivery, and

don't shy away from using rhetorical devices.
When you learn to use language purposefully,
you'll craft messages that stick, making a real
impact.

But hey, influence isn't just about you. Social
proof and authority matter big time. Use
testimonials, case studies, and your own
expertise to build credibility. In a world where
folks look to their peers for validation,
recommendations pack a punch.

Then there's reciprocity—a classic principle.
It's all about giving. Small acts can lead to
bigger commitments. When you create a vibe of
mutual benefit, you build relationships that last
and have real influence.

Scarcity and urgency are powerful motivators.
Everyone hates the idea of missing out (FOMO,
anyone?). Frame your offers to highlight how

limited they are, and watch your audience jump

into action.

Let's not forget cognitive biases. These quirks

in how we think can shape decisions. Spot

common biases, and you can either counter

them or use them to your advantage, boosting

your persuasive game.

Emotions drive a lot of our choices. If you can

tap into emotional triggers, you'll strike a

balance between logic and feeling, making your

message hit home on multiple levels. Know

what stirs your audience's emotions, and you'll

craft messages that inspire action and build

connections.

Nonverbal cues are another piece of the

puzzle. Body language, facial expressions, and

gestures can really amp up your

communication. When your words and body

language sync up, it creates a seamless experience that reinforces what you're saying.

How you frame your message matters, too. The way you present info can change how it's perceived. Get the context right and use positive framing, and you'll boost engagement and receptiveness.

Consistency is key. Getting people to commit to small things can lead to bigger commitments later. Understand the psychology behind commitment, and you'll create a persuasive strategy that builds trust and loyalty.

When it comes to negotiation, knowing the interests behind positions helps you find win-win solutions. This not only boosts your persuasive skills but also strengthens relationships.

Objections? They're part of the game. Anticipate concerns and tackle them with empathy. Turn objections into chances for connection. By reframing worries and showing value, you can build bridges that lead to success.

Finally, measuring your influence is crucial for growth. Keep track of what works and use feedback to refine your approach. Celebrate your wins and learn from the misses. This will help you navigate the ever-changing world of influence with confidence.

This book is your roadmap to mastering influence. As you dive into this journey, you'll discover principles that will elevate your marketing, sales, and communication skills. The power to persuade is in you—let's unlock it together!

Table of Contents

Chapter 1

The Foundations of Influence

Understanding the psychology behind influence is like peering into the very heart of human interaction. It's a captivating dance, one that unfolds daily in our lives. From the moment we rise to the time we settle in for the night, we are surrounded by choices, messages, and opinions that shape our decisions. If you're eager to master the art of persuasion, it's essential to grasp what truly drives people.

At the core of influence lies a fundamental truth: people are emotional beings. We often like to believe we're rational, logical creatures, but let's be honest. Our emotions frequently guide our choices. Think back to your last purchase. Was it purely a logical decision? More likely, it was fueled by joy, excitement, or perhaps a wave of nostalgia.

So, how do you tap into this rich emotional landscape? Start by asking the right questions. What fears haunt your audience? What dreams stir their hearts at night? What do they yearn for? By delving into these questions, you're not merely skimming the surface; you're exploring the depths of your audience's psyche. This understanding empowers you to craft messages that resonate on a personal level, igniting that emotional spark that drives action.

Now, let's shine a light on trust. It's the cornerstone of persuasion. Without trust, your

words become mere echoes in a bustling room.
Reflect on the last time someone attempted to
sell you something. If trust was absent, chances
are you turned away. Trust is cultivated over
time through consistency, transparency, and
authentic connection.

When you engage with your audience,
embrace authenticity. Share your story. Allow
yourself to be vulnerable. Let them see the real
you. People connect with individuals, not
faceless brands or rehearsed pitches. By
showing up as your true self, you forge a bond
that's difficult to break. And that bond? It
transforms skeptics into believers.

But here's the twist: trust isn't solely about
you. It's also about how you present your
message. You need to tune into your audience's
needs and desires. What are they searching for?
What challenges are they facing? By identifying

these elements, you can tailor your approach to
meet them where they are.

Picture yourself at a party. You wouldn't
just stride up to someone and launch into a
monologue about your favorite obscure hobby.
Instead, you'd seek common ground—perhaps
by asking about their interests or sharing a
lighthearted story. The same principle applies to
influence. You must engage your audience in a
manner that resonates with their experiences
and aspirations.

Once you've grasped their needs, begin
weaving your message around those insights.
It's akin to crafting a beautiful tapestry, where
each thread symbolizes a different desire or
concern. When your audience recognizes that
you truly understand them, they are far more
likely to listen. They'll feel seen and heard, and
that's an incredibly powerful connection.

Let's break this down into actionable steps.
First, immerse yourself in the psychology of
your audience. Conduct surveys, initiate
conversations, and do your research. What
motivates them? What keeps them awake at
night? Next, focus on building trust. Be
genuine, be transparent, and share your journey.
Remember, people yearn to connect with a real
person, not a polished persona.

Finally, pinpoint their needs and desires.
What are they after? What problems can you
help them resolve? By aligning your message
with their interests, you're not merely selling a
product or idea; you're offering a solution.
You're demonstrating that you understand their
world and are here to assist.

As you embark on this journey of mastering
influence, keep in mind that it's not solely about
reaching an end goal. It's about the connections
you forge along the way. Embrace the process,

celebrate the small victories, and keep moving forward. You've got this! Your words possess the power to change lives, and that's a truly beautiful thing.

In the end, the foundations of influence rest on understanding its psychology, building trust, and identifying your audience's needs and desires. When you weave these elements together, you create a powerful tapestry of influence that can elevate your marketing, sales, and communication strategies to new heights. So, roll up your sleeves, dive in, and let your journey begin!

Chapter 2

The Magic of Storytelling

Storytelling is where the real magic happens, folks. It's that invisible thread connecting us all, weaving through our lives. It's not just about sharing info; it's about taking your audience on a journey they won't forget. So, let's jump into the art of storytelling and see how you can use it to influence and persuade.

First up, let's chat about creating those killer narratives. Picture a story like a tasty sandwich. You've got your bread—the beginning and end—holding it all together. The juicy stuff in the middle? That's where the magic is. Your story needs a solid structure: a hook to grab attention, a conflict that resonates with your audience, and a resolution that leaves them feeling something—maybe inspired or enlightened.

Think about a personal experience you can share. Maybe it's a tough challenge you faced. You want your audience to feel like they're right there with you. Use vivid imagery. Instead of saying, "I was nervous before my big presentation," go for, "My heart raced like a wild horse as I peeked out at the sea of faces waiting for me." That's storytelling at its best.

Next, let's add some emotional spice. You want your audience to feel something—joy, sadness, excitement, or even anger. Emotions are what keep people engaged. When you tap into feelings, you're not just talking; you're connecting. Think back to a story that really moved you. Was it a movie, a book, or a deep chat? What made it hit home? Usually, it's that emotional truth that resonates.

Here's a fun exercise: write down the emotions you want your audience to feel. Hopeful? Empowered? Challenged? Once you've got your list, recall moments in your life that stirred those feelings. Jot them down! These anecdotes will add authenticity to your narrative, making it relatable.

But wait, there's more! The structure of your story is key. You want to keep folks engaged from start to finish. Think of your story as a rollercoaster ride. You start with a thrilling climb, build up the tension, and then hit that exhilarating drop that keeps everyone glued to their seats.

A classic way to structure a story is the three-act format: setup, confrontation, and resolution. In the setup, introduce your characters and their world. In the confrontation, lay out the challenge or conflict they face. And in the resolution, show how they tackle that challenge and what they learn. This keeps your story easy to follow and ensures your audience is invested.

As you tell your tale, don't forget those sensory details. What did the air smell like? How did the ground feel? What sounds were around you? These details help your audience step into your shoes and experience the story with you. Engaging their senses creates a vivid picture that sticks in their minds long after you're done.

Now, let's think about the impact your storytelling can have. When you share a story that resonates, you're not just swaying opinions;

you're changing lives. You're offering new perspectives, inspiring action, or encouraging folks to tackle their own challenges. That's a powerful gift you have as a storyteller.

Feeling stuck? Writer's block got you down? No worries! Here's a trick: try freewriting. Set a timer for ten minutes and just write—don't stop for grammar or coherence. Let your thoughts flow. You might stumble upon some gems that spark fresh ideas for your story.

Every great storyteller started somewhere. Embrace your unique voice and perspective. Your experiences are yours alone, and that's what makes your story shine. Don't shy away from vulnerability; those raw, honest moments often resonate the most. Your audience will appreciate your authenticity and connect with your message.

As we wrap this up, visualize your success. Picture your audience hanging on your every word, nodding along, feeling inspired by your story. Imagine the ripple effect your narrative will create in their lives. That's the beauty of storytelling—it's not just about you; it's about the impact you make in the world.

So, dive into the art of storytelling. Craft those compelling narratives, tap into emotions, and structure your stories to captivate your audience. You've got this! The world is ready to hear your tales, and I can't wait to see how you influence and inspire with your words. Remember, storytelling is a journey, and every word you write brings you closer to making a difference. Let's get to it!

Chapter 3

Building Rapport

When it comes to persuasion, it's all about the connections we make. Building rapport? It's not just a buzzword; it's the core of solid communication. Think of it as a bridge that links you to your audience—a strong one that lets trust flow. Let's jump into some tricks for creating that vital connection. Trust me, when you connect, you influence.

First up, genuine interest is key. When you approach someone with an open heart and curiosity, it's like tossing a lifeline in a sea of apathy. Ask questions that show you care, like, "What's been the best part of your week?" or "What's your current passion project?" These kinds of questions spark conversation and prove you're not just there to push your agenda. You're there to engage, listen, and really understand.

Now, let's talk about active listening. This isn't just about hearing the words; it's about digging into the emotions behind them. Picture this: you're chatting, and instead of just waiting to speak, you lean in, nod, and reflect back what you hear. "So, you felt overwhelmed at work but found a way to handle it?" This simple act validates their feelings and tightens your bond.

Active listening is like a dance. You move with your partner, responding to their cues and adjusting your steps. It's about creating a rhythm where both sides feel heard and valued.

When folks feel listened to, they're more likely
to open up and trust you. And trust? That's the
golden ticket to persuasion.

But wait, there's more! Let's throw in
another layer: mirroring and matching. You
might think, "Isn't that a bit sneaky?" Nope! It's
a natural human thing that happens when we
vibe with someone. When you subtly mimic the
other person's body language, tone, or even
how fast they talk, it creates familiarity. It's like
saying, "Hey, we're on the same page!"

Imagine you're in a meeting, and your
colleague leans back, arms crossed. Instead of
sitting stiffly, you relax a bit too. Or if they
speak softly, you lower your voice. This isn't
about being fake; it's about building a
connection. People are drawn to those who
mirror them because it creates a sense of
understanding and camaraderie.

But let's be clear—this isn't about imitation. It's a dance of empathy. You want to be real while tuning into the other person's vibe. If they're excited and animated, match that energy! If they're calm and reflective, slow it down. Balancing mirroring with authenticity makes communication powerful.

Now, let's wrap this up with a little motivation. Building rapport is like planting seeds in a garden. It takes time, patience, and care, but when those seeds sprout, they grow into strong relationships that can weather any storm. Each connection you make opens doors to influence, collaboration, and shared success.

So, as you move forward, keep these techniques in mind. Engage with genuine interest, listen actively, and embrace the art of mirroring. You've got the tools to create lasting connections that will boost your marketing, sales, and communication game.

Now, go out there and start building those bridges! Your influence is waiting.

Chapter 4

The Power of Language

Words pack a punch, don't they? They can connect people or tear them apart. If you wanna persuade someone, it's all about picking the right words—those that spark action, fuel passion, and touch hearts. Think of your words like seeds. When you plant 'em in the right spot, they can bloom into something amazing. So, how do you pick words that hit home?

First, nail down your message. What feelings do you want to stir in your audience? What action should they take? Use vivid language that paints a clear picture. Instead of "help," go for "empower." Swap "buy now" for "join the movement." Those words pack more emotion and urgency. They invite folks to be part of something bigger.

Now, let's chat about tone and delivery. Picture yourself at a family cookout. You wouldn't shout across the yard, right? You'd lean in, maybe share a laugh. That's what tone is all about. It's not just the words; it's how you say 'em. Your tone can show warmth, excitement, or authority. When you deliver your message with the right vibe, you create a connection.

Think back to a time when a speech or piece of writing really moved you. Bet it wasn't just the words—it was the delivery. The pauses, the emphasis, the passion behind 'em. When you speak or write, let your personality shine. If you're pumped, let that excitement flow. If it's serious, let that gravity pull in your audience. They'll feel it, and they're more likely to engage.

Now, let's jazz things up with rhetorical devices. These are the secret sauce that can turn your message from meh to wow. Metaphors, similes, alliteration—these tools can make your words sing. Instead of saying "act fast," try "this opportunity is a shooting star—blink, and it's gone."

Rhetorical questions? Total game-changer. They pull your audience in and get 'em thinking. "Isn't it time you took charge of your future?" You're not just stating a fact; you're nudging them to reflect. It's like a gentle push toward the conclusion you want them to reach.

Repetition is another killer tactic. It's simple but effective. Think about Martin Luther King

Jr.'s iconic "I have a dream" speech. That phrase sticks, right? The repetition creates a rhythm that resonates. When you hammer home key phrases, you reinforce your message and make it memorable.

And let's not forget storytelling. We've touched on this before, but it bears repeating. Stories are the heartbeat of communication. They make your message relatable and unforgettable. When you share a personal tale or an anecdote that connects to your main point, you're not just informing; you're inviting your audience into your world. They can see themselves in your story, and that's where the magic happens.

So, as you craft your message, remember to choose words that inspire action, deliver 'em with the right tone, and sprinkle in some rhetorical devices to elevate your message.

Here's a little exercise for ya: Grab
something you've written recently—an email, a
blog post, or even a speech. Read it out loud.
Notice the words you've picked and how you
deliver 'em. Do they inspire action? Is your tone
engaging? Are you using any rhetorical tricks?

Once you've taken a good look, jot down
three words you can swap for stronger ones.
Then, find a spot where you can throw in a story
or a rhetorical question.

You got this! Remember, language is a
powerful tool. You can inspire, motivate, and
persuade. Embrace it, and watch your words
create waves of change around you.

And hey, practice makes perfect. The more
you mess around with language, the more
natural it'll feel. So, keep writing, keep talking,
and keep believing in your voice. You're on a

journey, and every word you choose gets you closer to making a real impact.

So, what's holding you back? Get out there and let your words soar!

Chapter 5

Social Proof and Authority

When it comes to persuading folks, let me tell ya, social proof and authority are like the secret sauce in a grandma's famous recipe— absolutely essential! Think about it: we humans are social creatures. We look to others for guidance, especially when we're uncertain. So, how can you tap into this natural tendency? Let's dive into the magic of testimonials, the power of expertise, and the sway of peer recommendations. You'll see how these elements can elevate your marketing, sales, and communication strategies to a whole new level.

First off, let's chat about testimonials and case studies. Picture this: you're standing in a crowded room, and you hear someone rave about a product or service. Their excitement is contagious, right? That's the essence of testimonials. They act like a warm hug on a cold day—comforting and reassuring. When potential customers see that others have had positive experiences, it builds trust and credibility.

Now, don't just collect any old testimonials. Go for the gold! Seek out stories that resonate with your target audience. If you're selling a fitness program, find someone who transformed their life and can share their journey. A heartfelt story that showcases real results can be more persuasive than a thousand ads.

But how do you leverage these testimonials effectively? Well, sprinkle them throughout your marketing materials. Use them in emails, on your website, and in social media posts. Create case studies that tell a compelling story, detailing the challenges faced, the solutions provided, and the triumphant outcomes. Make it relatable. When people see someone like them achieving success, it sparks hope and motivation. They start thinking, "If they can do it, so can I!"

Now, let's pivot a bit and talk about establishing credibility through expertise. You want to be seen as the go-to person in your field, right? It's all about positioning yourself as an authority. This doesn't mean you need to be a walking encyclopedia, but you should have a solid understanding of your subject matter. Share your knowledge! Write articles, give talks, or host webinars. The more you put yourself out there, the more people will recognize your expertise.

Think of it this way: when you see someone wearing a lab coat, you instinctively trust them, don't you? That's the power of authority. You can create that same effect by showcasing your qualifications, experiences, and successes. Maybe you've written a book, or you've got years of experience under your belt. Don't be shy—share it! Create a strong personal brand that reflects your expertise.

And here's a little secret: don't just talk about your achievements; highlight the achievements of those you've helped. When people see that you've guided others to success, it reinforces your credibility. It's like having a badge of honor that says, "I know what I'm talking about, and I've got the results to prove it!"

Now, let's not forget about the influence of peer recommendations. Word-of-mouth is a powerful force. Think about it—when was the last time you made a purchase based on a friend's recommendation? It happens all the time! People trust their peers more than they trust ads. So, how can you harness this power?

Start by encouraging satisfied customers to spread the word. Offer incentives for referrals or create a loyalty program that rewards them for bringing in new clients. You might even consider hosting events or workshops where your current customers can invite friends. This not only builds community but also fosters an environment where recommendations can flourish.

Another effective strategy is to engage with influencers in your niche. These are the folks who've already built a following and have the trust of their audience. If they endorse your product or service, it's like getting a golden ticket to credibility. But remember, authenticity is key. Choose influencers who align with your

values and whose audience matches your target
market.

As you weave these elements together—
testimonials, expertise, and peer
recommendations—you're creating a tapestry of
trust. It's like building a sturdy bridge that
connects you to your audience. They'll feel
more inclined to listen to you, to engage with
your offerings, and ultimately, to take action.

Now, let's get a bit practical here. Here are a
few steps you can take to incorporate social
proof and authority into your strategy:

1. Collect and showcase testimonials
regularly. Make it a habit to ask for feedback
after every successful interaction. Use tools like
Google Forms or SurveyMonkey to gather
insights easily.

2. Create case studies that tell compelling
stories. Use a simple format: challenge,
solution, and result. Make it visually appealing
with images and graphs if possible.

3. Position yourself as an expert. Write
articles, start a blog, or even create a podcast.
Share your insights and experiences to build
your authority.

4. Encourage word-of-mouth marketing.
Implement a referral program that rewards
customers for bringing in new clients.

5. Collaborate with influencers. Reach out to
those who resonate with your brand and explore
partnership opportunities.

6. Keep your audience engaged. Use social media to share testimonials, case studies, and expert insights regularly.

Remember, building social proof and authority takes time, but the rewards are worth it. You're not just selling a product or service; you're building a community of trust and connection.

So, as you embark on this journey, keep your chin up and your heart open. You have the power to influence, to inspire, and to create change. Embrace the process, celebrate your small wins, and know that every step you take brings you closer to your goals.

Now go out there and make your mark! Your voice matters, and the world is waiting to hear what you have to say.

Chapter 6

The Principle of Reciprocity

Creating a culture of giving is like planting seeds in a garden. You gotta nurture those seeds, water 'em, and give 'em sunlight. When you create an environment where giving is the norm, you not only enrich the soil but also cultivate a thriving community. It's about fostering a spirit of generosity that ripples through your relationships, be it in business, friendships, or family.

Think about it: when you give, you create a bond. It's that simple. You're not just handing over a favor or a kind word; you're establishing

a connection. And connections? They're the
lifeblood of influence. When people feel valued
and appreciated, they're more likely to
reciprocate. It's like a dance—one step forward,
one step back, and before you know it, you're
moving in harmony.

Now, let's break it down a bit. Small
gestures can lead to larger commitments. You
ever hold the door open for someone? It's a
simple act, but it can make a big difference.
That little moment of kindness can spark a sense
of obligation, even if it's unspoken. People tend
to feel compelled to return the favor, whether
it's through a smile, a thank you, or even a more
significant commitment down the line.

Picture this: you're at a networking event,
and you take a moment to genuinely listen to
someone's story. You ask questions, show
interest, and before you know it, they're
opening up about their challenges and

aspirations. That small gesture of attentiveness builds trust. And trust? That's the foundation of any meaningful relationship. When you invest in others, they're more likely to invest back in you.

Building lasting relationships through mutual benefit is where the magic happens. It's not just about one person giving while the other takes. It's about creating a cycle of generosity that benefits everyone involved. When both parties feel they're gaining something from the relationship, it transforms into a partnership.

Take a moment to reflect on your own life. Think about the people you're closest to. I bet those relationships are built on a foundation of give-and-take. Maybe you helped a friend move, and in return, they treated you to dinner. Or perhaps you offered your expertise on a project, and later, they provided you with a valuable introduction. Those mutual benefits

strengthen your bond and make the relationship
more resilient.

Now, let's talk strategy. You can actively
create this culture of giving by incorporating
small, thoughtful gestures into your daily
interactions. It could be as simple as sending a
handwritten note to a colleague, offering to help
someone with a task, or sharing a resource that
could benefit them. These acts don't have to be
grand or expensive; it's the thought and
intention behind them that counts.

Here's a little exercise for you: make a list
of five people in your life—friends, family,
colleagues, anyone who comes to mind. Next to
each name, jot down a small gesture you could
offer them. It could be a compliment, a helping
hand, or even just checking in to see how
they're doing. Set a goal to complete at least
one gesture for each person within the next

week. Trust me, you'll feel great, and you'll likely spark a little reciprocity in return.

Remember, the principle of reciprocity isn't just about getting something back. It's about creating a culture where everyone feels valued and supported. When you give, you're not just investing in others; you're investing in yourself. You're building a network of support that can uplift you when you need it most.

Now, let's wrap this up with a little motivation. You have the power to influence those around you, to create a community of giving and receiving. Every small gesture you make is a step toward building deeper, more meaningful relationships. So, get out there and start planting those seeds. You never know how they might grow!

The beauty of reciprocity lies in its simplicity. It's a cycle of kindness that can transform your life and the lives of those around you. Embrace it, nurture it, and watch as your connections flourish. You got this!

Chapter 7

Scarcity and Urgency

Ever been in a store and spotted a sign that screams, "Only 3 left!"? Or got an email saying, "This offer ends at midnight!"? That little jolt you feel? That's scarcity and urgency working their magic. It's a psychological nudge that pushes us to act fast, to snatch that item before it vanishes. When you tap into limited availability, you're not just stirring up excitement—you're driving action.

Let's break this down. When folks see something as scarce, it suddenly feels more valuable. Picture this: if you know there are

only a few spots left for a workshop or a
limited-edition product, what do you feel? That
gut tug—the fear of missing out. Enter FOMO.
It's that nagging sensation that if you don't
jump in quickly, you'll be left behind while
everyone else enjoys the perks.

So, how do you whip up a call to action that
capitalizes on this? First, clarity's your best
buddy. You gotta make it crystal clear what you
want your audience to do and why they should
do it now. A killer call to action is like a neon
sign in a dark alley—impossible to ignore.
Phrases like "Join now before it's too late!" or
"Claim your spot today!" work wonders. They
create urgency and shout that action's needed—
like, ASAP.

But here's the kicker: your scarcity can't
just be a gimmick. Authenticity matters. If you
say there are only a few spots left, there better
be. If you set a deadline, stick to it. Your

audience needs to trust you. Trust is the bedrock of influence, and if they feel duped, that trust will vanish quicker than a summer storm.

Now, let's paint a picture. Imagine launching a new online course. You've poured your heart into it, and now it's time to share it. You send out an email announcing the launch, but here's the twist: the first 50 sign-ups get an exclusive bonus—maybe a one-on-one coaching session with you. Suddenly, that course isn't just a course; it's a golden ticket, and those 50 spots are hot commodities. People scramble to secure their spot 'cause they don't wanna miss out on that extra value.

But wait, there's more! You can crank up that urgency by adding a deadline. "Sign up by Friday at midnight to snag your bonus!" Now there's a ticking clock. As the deadline approaches, anxiety kicks in. FOMO creeps up, and before you know it, they're clicking that sign-up button faster than kids in a candy store.

Now, let's chat about your language. Your words matter. They should spark emotions and excitement. Instead of saying, "We have limited spots available," try something like, "Only a handful of spots remain—don't let this chance slip away!" It's all about painting a vivid picture. Make 'em feel the thrill of what they could gain and the disappointment of what they might lose.

And here's a little secret: people love feeling special. Frame your offer as exclusive, and you'll heighten that desire. Use phrases like "Join an elite group of achievers" or "Be among the first to experience this life-changing program." You're not just selling; you're inviting them into a community, a movement.

But keep it real. Scarcity and urgency are powerful tools, but they should align with your values and the true nature of what you're offering. If you promise something exclusive, deliver. If you set a deadline, honor it. Your audience will appreciate your honesty, and that appreciation builds loyalty.

So, let's recap. First, use limited availability to drive action. Make your audience feel that what you're offering is hot stuff. Second, tap into FOMO. Make 'em feel that if they don't act now, they might miss out on something amazing. Third, craft clear, urgent, and authentic calls to action. Use language that evokes emotion and creates a sense of belonging.

Now, take a moment to think about how you can apply this to your work. What opportunities do you have to create urgency? How can you frame your offerings as scarce and exclusive?

Here's a fun exercise: jot down your current projects or offerings. Next to each one, brainstorm how you can introduce an element of scarcity or urgency. Maybe it's a limited-time discount, an exclusive bonus for early sign-ups, or a countdown timer on your website. Get creative!

You've got this. The power of persuasion is in your hands. With the right strategies, you can inspire action and build meaningful connections with your audience. Embrace the journey, and watch your influence grow. You're not just selling a product; you're changing lives, one call to action at a time. Now go out there and make it happen!

Chapter 8

Understanding Cognitive Biases

Cognitive biases—those sneaky little shortcuts our brains take when making decisions. They can trip us up or give us a leg up, depending on how we wield them. Let's dive into this fascinating world and learn how to identify these biases, counteract them in our messaging, and even use them to our advantage in persuasion. Buckle up, my friend; we're about to embark on a journey through the mind!

First off, let's talk about identifying common biases that affect decision-making. You know how sometimes you make a choice and later wonder, "What was I thinking?" That's your brain's biases at play. One of the most prevalent biases is confirmation bias. This little rascal makes us seek out information that confirms our existing beliefs while ignoring evidence that contradicts them. It's like wearing blinders, only seeing what we want to see.

Then there's the anchoring bias. Picture this: you walk into a store, and the first item you see is priced at $100. Suddenly, everything else seems cheaper in comparison. That initial price has anchored your perception. It's a powerful tool that marketers often exploit. And let's not forget about the availability heuristic. This one's all about how recent experiences shape our judgments. If you hear about a plane crash on the news, you might overestimate the danger of flying, even though statistically, it's safer than driving.

Now that we've got a handle on some common biases, let's move on to strategies to counteract these biases in your messaging. You see, awareness is key. When you recognize that biases are at play, you can craft your message to cut through the noise.

Start by presenting balanced information. If you know your audience is likely to fall prey to confirmation bias, offer them data that challenges their beliefs. It's like a friendly nudge, encouraging them to consider a different perspective. You want to create a safe space for open dialogue. Use stories and examples that resonate with their experiences, but also sprinkle in some unexpected insights. This way, you're engaging their minds while gently guiding them to think differently.

Another powerful strategy is to leverage the power of social proof. Remember that anchoring bias? Well, if you can show that others—especially those they respect—have made a different choice, it can shift their perception. Testimonials, case studies, and endorsements from trusted figures can help recalibrate their decision-making process.

Now, let's get a bit more creative. Think about using visuals. Infographics and compelling images can bypass some of those cognitive shortcuts. They draw attention and can present complex information in a digestible way. When your audience sees something that resonates with them visually, it can break through the biases and make them more receptive to your message.

But here's the kicker—using biases to your advantage in persuasion. This is where the magic happens! Once you understand these biases, you can flip the script and harness them to influence your audience positively.

Take the scarcity principle, for instance.
People are wired to want what they can't have.
If you can create a sense of urgency around
your offering, it taps into that fear of missing
out (FOMO). Limited-time offers or exclusive
deals can trigger that emotional response,
making your audience more likely to act.

Another way to leverage cognitive biases is
through the framing effect. How you present
information can dramatically alter how it's
perceived. For example, instead of saying, "This
product has a 90% success rate," you might say,
"Only 10% of users didn't achieve their desired
results." Same information, different framing.
It's all about how you position your message.

And let's not forget about the power of
storytelling. We've touched on this before, but
it bears repeating. Crafting narratives that
resonate with your audience's experiences can
bypass those cognitive biases. When they see

themselves in your story, it creates an emotional connection that can be far more persuasive than cold hard facts.

As we wrap up this exploration of cognitive biases, remember that understanding these mental shortcuts is like having a secret weapon in your persuasion toolkit. You've got the power to identify biases, counteract them in your messaging, and even turn them to your advantage.

So, take a moment to reflect on your own experiences. Think about the times you've made decisions based on biases—both in yourself and in others. How can you use this knowledge to elevate your marketing, sales, and communication strategies?

Here's a practical exercise for you: Make a list of three cognitive biases you've noticed in

your own decision-making or in your audience.
For each bias, brainstorm a strategy to
counteract it in your messaging. Then, think
about how you might leverage those biases to
enhance your persuasion techniques.

Remember, this isn't just about influencing
others; it's about creating genuine connections
and fostering understanding. You're not just a
marketer or a salesperson; you're a guide,
helping others navigate their choices with
clarity and purpose.

So, get out there and embrace the power of
cognitive biases. Use them wisely, and watch as
your influence grows, not just in your
professional life, but in every interaction you
have. You've got this!

Chapter 9

Emotional Appeals

Emotions are the heartbeat of communication. When you tap into them, you're not just talking; you're connecting. Think about it—when you hear a story that stirs your heart, or a message that resonates deep within, it's like the world fades away, and all that matters is that moment. Harnessing the power of emotions in your communication can transform your words from mere sentences into a symphony of influence.

Now, let's dive into how you can wield this power effectively. First off, it's crucial to balance logic and emotion. Too much logic can make your message feel cold, like a winter's day without a hint of sunshine. On the flip side, if you lean too heavily on emotions, your message might come off as lacking substance. It's a dance, my friend—a beautiful tango between the heart and the mind.

So, how do you find that sweet spot? Start by knowing your audience. What makes them tick? What keeps them up at night? Identifying emotional triggers is your golden ticket here. These triggers are like little keys that unlock your audience's hearts. Maybe it's the fear of failure, the desire for belonging, or the joy of success. When you understand what moves them, you can tailor your message to resonate deeply.

Picture this: you're in a room full of people,
and you want to inspire them. You could throw
a bunch of statistics at them, but let's be
honest—numbers can be as dry as toast. Instead,
share a story. Share a moment that evokes a
feeling. When you weave emotion into your
narrative, you create a connection that logic
alone can't achieve.

Now, don't get me wrong—logic has its
place. It's like the sturdy foundation of a house.
You need it to support the emotional roof you're
building. Use facts and figures to back up your
claims, but do it in a way that complements the
emotional appeal. For instance, if you're
discussing the importance of a product, don't
just list its features. Share a story about
someone whose life changed because of it.
Show how it brought them joy, relief, or hope.

As you craft your message, think about the
emotional journey you want to take your

audience on. What do you want them to feel? How do you want them to react? You can guide them through this journey by carefully choosing your words and the stories you tell. Use vivid imagery, relatable anecdotes, and heartfelt language. Make them laugh, make them cry, but most importantly, make them feel.

Remember, the goal is to create a connection. When your audience feels something, they're more likely to act. They'll remember your message, and they'll be moved to share it with others. That's the magic of emotional appeals—it's not just about influencing one person; it's about creating a ripple effect.

So, how do you identify those emotional triggers? Start by doing your homework. Get to know your audience. Conduct surveys, read their comments, or engage in conversations. Pay attention to the language they use. What words do they choose when they talk about their challenges and dreams? These insights will help you craft messages that resonate.

Once you've identified those triggers, it's time to put them to work. Think about how you can incorporate them into your communication strategy. For example, if you know your audience fears missing out, use that to your advantage. Create a sense of urgency in your messaging. Let them know that your solution is the key to overcoming their fears and achieving their desires.

But let's not forget the power of vulnerability. Sharing your own emotional experiences can create an authentic connection with your audience. It shows them you're human, just like them. You've faced struggles, and you've come out the other side. This transparency can be incredibly powerful in persuading others to take action.

As you navigate the delicate balance of emotion and logic, keep in mind that authenticity is key. Don't force emotions; let them flow naturally. Your audience can sense when something feels contrived. Speak from the heart, and your message will resonate on a deeper level.

In closing, emotional appeals are a vital part of effective persuasion. By harnessing the power of emotions, balancing them with logic, and identifying your audience's emotional triggers, you can create messages that inspire action and drive change. So go ahead, embrace the emotional side of communication. It's where the real magic happens.

Remember, you've got this! You're not just a writer; you're a storyteller, a communicator, a bridge between ideas and hearts. Each word you write has the potential to change lives. So, take a deep breath, dive into those emotions, and let your message soar!

Chapter 10

Nonverbal Communication

You've heard the saying, "actions speak louder than words," right? Well, when it comes to influencing others, that's spot on. Nonverbal communication is like the secret ingredient in your persuasive arsenal. It's all about body language, facial expressions, and gestures that can either back up what you're saying or throw it all outta whack. Think of it like the melody to your lyrics. If they're off-key, folks will be left confused, scratching their heads, wondering what you really mean.

Let's dig into body language and its role in
influence. Picture this: you're in a crowded
room, trying to pitch your amazing idea. You
could have the slickest words ready, but if your
body language is saying something else, it's like
trying to sell ice to an Eskimo while you're
bundled up in a parka. Your posture,
movements, and how you position your arms
send strong signals. Are you open and
approachable, or are you closed off and
defensive? Standing tall with your shoulders
back? Or hunched over, looking like you'd
rather be anywhere else?

When you carry yourself with confidence, it
doesn't just make you look good; it makes
people more likely to listen. They can feel your
energy—it's magnetic. You wanna be that
person who walks into a room and grabs
attention without even saying a word. So,
practice those power poses! Stand like you own
the place. It'll boost your confidence and send a
message that you mean business.

Now, let's chat about facial expressions and gestures. Your face is like a canvas, and every smile, frown, or raised eyebrow tells a story. Ever notice how a genuine smile can brighten up a room? It's infectious! When you smile, you're not just showing warmth; you're inviting others to relax and engage. On the flip side, a furrowed brow or crossed arms can scream skepticism or defensiveness.

Gestures matter too. A well-timed hand movement can highlight a point and make it stick in people's minds. But watch out—too many wild gestures can distract from your message. Think of your hands as trusty sidekicks, backing up your words without stealing the spotlight. Practice in front of a mirror. See what feels natural and what looks like a windmill caught in a storm.

And we can't overlook the magic of aligning verbal and nonverbal messages. When your words and body language sync up, it's like a symphony playing in perfect harmony. People feel it deep down. They trust you more. But if there's a mismatch? That raises red flags. Imagine telling someone how excited you are about a project while your arms are crossed and your face looks like you just bit into a sour lemon. Confusion kicks in. Do you really mean it?

To create that alignment, you've gotta be mindful. Before diving into a convo, check in with yourself. What's your body saying? Are you projecting confidence? Are you genuinely excited? Your nonverbal cues should reflect your message. If you're passionate about what you're saying, let it shine through your body language. Lean in a bit, use your hands to illustrate your points, and let that enthusiasm radiate.

Here's a fun exercise: next time you're chatting with someone, pay attention to their nonverbal signals. What's their body language telling you? Are they engaged, or are they zoning out? This'll sharpen your observational skills and help you tweak your own nonverbal cues to connect better with them.

And don't forget self-awareness. Your nonverbal communication reflects your inner state. If you're anxious, it'll show. So, take a breath, ground yourself, and channel that energy into positive body language. It's a game changer.

As we wrap this up, remember: nonverbal communication is your ally in persuasion. It's that silent partner that can amplify your message or send it crashing down. Be intentional with your body language, embrace the power of your facial expressions, and align

your verbal and nonverbal messages like a
finely tuned orchestra.

You've got the tools to make a lasting
impact. Go out there and wield them with
confidence. Your words matter, but your
presence matters even more. Own it, embrace it,
and watch how it transforms your interactions.
You're on your way to mastering the
psychology of influence, one gesture at a time.

Chapter 11

Framing Your Message

Alright, my friend, let's dive into the art of framing your message. This is where the magic happens—where you take the raw materials of your ideas and shape 'em into something that resonates. You know how a good frame can make a picture pop? Well, the same goes for your words. How you present information can make all the difference in the world.

First off, let's talk about presenting information for maximum impact. Imagine you're at a dinner party, and someone starts talking about their recent trip to the Grand Canyon. If they drone on and on, you might find yourself staring at your plate, right? But if they start with a vivid description—the colors of the sunset, the vastness of the canyon, the thrill of standing on the edge—suddenly, you're leaning in, hanging on every word. That's the power of presentation.

To create that kind of engagement, focus on three key elements: clarity, relevance, and emotion. Keep your message clear and concise. Don't clutter it with jargon or unnecessary details. Your audience should grasp your main point without having to sift through a mountain of words. Relevance is equally important. Tailor your message to the interests and needs of your audience. If they're business-minded folks, relate your ideas to profit margins or market trends. If they're creative types, appeal to their artistic sensibilities. And don't forget about emotion! People remember how you made them feel far more than the facts you presented. So, tap into those feelings—whether it's excitement, nostalgia, or even a touch of humor.

Now, let's shift gears and talk about context. Context is like the backdrop of a stage—it sets the scene for your message. Without it, your audience might feel lost, like they're wandering in a fog. You want to paint a picture that gives your audience a frame of reference.

Consider this: you're pitching a new product. If you simply throw out the features and benefits, it might not land as you hoped. But if you start by sharing a relatable story about a problem people face, then introduce your product as the solution, you've given your audience the context they need to understand and appreciate your message. It's all about creating a narrative that wraps around your ideas and makes them feel relevant and urgent.

Remember, context also involves understanding the environment in which you're communicating. Is it a formal presentation, a casual chat over coffee, or a social media post? Each setting calls for a different approach. Adapt your framing to fit the situation, and you'll find your audience more receptive to what you have to say.

And speaking of receptiveness, let's dive into the power of positive framing. This is where you can really elevate your message. Positive framing is all about presenting your ideas in a way that highlights the benefits and possibilities rather than the drawbacks or limitations. It's like looking at the glass as half full instead of half empty.

For example, instead of saying, "This program will save you time," try, "Imagine what you could achieve with those extra hours!" See how that shifts the focus? You're not just stating a fact; you're inviting your audience to visualize the positive outcomes of your proposal. It's a subtle but powerful shift that can make your message more compelling.

Another effective technique is to use "we" language instead of "you" language. When you say, "You can achieve your goals," it puts the onus on the listener. But when you say, "Together, we can achieve our goals," it fosters a sense of partnership and collaboration. You're inviting them into the journey, and that's a powerful motivator.

So, as you craft your message, keep these principles in mind. Present your information with clarity and relevance, provide the necessary context, and frame it positively. This trifecta will not only enhance the impact of your message but also create a deeper connection with your audience.

And remember, every time you share your ideas, you're not just talking at people—you're opening a dialogue. You're inviting them to be part of something bigger. So, take a moment to visualize the impact your words can have. Picture your audience leaning in, nodding along, and feeling inspired by what you have to say.

Now, let's put this into action. Take a moment to jot down a key message you want to share. Think about how you can present it for maximum impact. What's the most engaging way to frame it? What context can you provide to make it relatable? And how can you infuse positivity into your framing?

Once you've got that down, practice it out loud. See how it feels. Adjust your tone, your pacing, and your body language. You're not just a messenger; you're a storyteller, a guide, and a source of inspiration. Embrace that role and let your passion shine through.

As you continue on this journey of mastering persuasion, remember that every interaction is an opportunity. An opportunity to connect, to inspire, and to create change. You've got the tools; now it's time to use them. Go out there and frame your message with power! You've got this!

Chapter 12

The Role of Consistency

When you think about persuasion, consistency is like the sturdy backbone of a tree—solid and dependable. The trick to getting people on board with your ideas or products often kicks off with small agreements. Imagine this: if you can snag a "yes" for a tiny favor, they're way more likely to agree to something bigger down the line. It's kinda like planting a seed; with a bit of care, that little seed can blossom into something amazing.

Now, let's unpack the psychology behind commitment and consistency. Ever heard of the foot-in-the-door technique? It's a classic move! Picture this: you ask your neighbor to sign a petition for a local cause. They say yes. Later, you swing by again and ask if they'd host a small gathering to chat about the same cause. Odds are, they'll agree again. Why? People have this deep-rooted urge to stay consistent with their past actions. It's a powerful motivator and can really amp up your persuasive game.

So, how do you craft a persuasive strategy that leans on consistency? First things first, start small. Think baby steps. You wanna create a chain of little commitments that lead to a bigger ask. This could be as easy as getting someone to follow you on social media before hitting them up to subscribe to your newsletter. Each little "yes" builds up momentum, making them feel kinda obligated to go along with bigger requests later.

Next up, frame those small agreements in a way that clicks with your audience's values and beliefs. If your crowd cares about community, present your requests in a way that highlights their role in making a difference. "By signing this petition, you're helping our community thrive!" This way, you're not just asking for a favor; you're inviting them to join something bigger.

But remember, consistency isn't just about racking up "yeses." It's about building a relationship where they feel good about their choices. Celebrate those small wins! When someone agrees to a small request, thank them and recognize their commitment. This reinforces their decision and makes them more likely to say "yes" again in the future.

And don't overlook the power of storytelling. Sharing personal stories or relatable examples creates a connection. This bond

fosters trust and makes it easier for your
audience to commit to your ideas. Maybe
you've got a tale about how a small choice
turned your life around. That not only drives
your point home but also shows your audience
the potential impact of their own small
commitments.

Now, let's chat about the importance of
consistency in your messaging. Your words,
tone, and actions should all vibe together. If
you're pushing a healthy lifestyle but your
message is all over the place, people are gonna
be confused. Consistency builds trust, and trust
is the bedrock of influence. So, make sure
you're walking the walk and talking the talk.

As you put together your persuasive
strategy, keep these key points in mind:

1. Start with small agreements. Get your audience to say "yes" to little things before moving to bigger requests.

2. Frame your asks to align with your audience's values. Make 'em feel like they're part of something meaningful.

3. Celebrate small wins! Acknowledge your audience's commitments and reinforce their choices.

4. Use storytelling to create connections. Share personal anecdotes that illustrate the impact of small decisions.

5. Ensure consistency in your messaging. Your words and actions should align to build trust.

Now, take a sec to think about the power of consistency in your own life. Recall a time when you made a small commitment that snowballed into something bigger. Maybe it was agreeing to attend a workshop that shifted your career. Or joining a book club that ignited a love for reading. Those little steps can lead to big changes.

As you continue your writing journey, keep in mind that consistency is crucial. Your readers crave guidance, and your knack for creating a persuasive strategy rooted in consistent messaging will not only elevate your work but also resonate with those who read it. You've got this! Embrace the ride, and let the power of consistency be your guiding star.

Chapter 13

Negotiation Tactics

Let's dive into the art of negotiation, shall we? It's like a dance, really—a back-and-forth rhythm where both partners need to feel the music. You want to get what you need, but you also want the other party to walk away feeling like they've gained something too. That's the sweet spot. So, how do we get there? Well, grab a seat and let's break it down.

First off, strategies for effective negotiation are your bread and butter. You gotta have a game plan. Think of it like prepping for a big game—know your plays, but be ready to adapt when the unexpected comes your way. Start by setting clear objectives. What do you want? What are you willing to give up? Write it down. Visualize it. When you have clarity on your goals, you can navigate the conversation like a seasoned pro.

Now, let's talk about understanding the interests behind positions. This is where things get juicy. People often come to the table with a position, like, "I want a raise" or "I need this deal to go through." But what's really behind that? What's driving those desires? Maybe it's financial security, recognition, or the need for validation. When you peel back those layers, you uncover the real motivations. This is where the magic happens.

Imagine you're negotiating a salary. Instead of just focusing on the number, ask yourself:

Why does this matter to them? Is it about feeling valued in the company? Maybe they're trying to set a precedent for future hires. When you understand their underlying interests, you can frame your proposal in a way that resonates with them. It's like tuning into the right radio station—suddenly, everything clicks.

Finding win-win solutions is the cherry on top of this negotiation sundae. It's about collaboration, not combat. Picture this: You're both in a room, and instead of trying to outmaneuver each other, you're brainstorming together. What can you offer that meets your needs while also satisfying theirs? This is where creativity shines.

Let's say you're negotiating a contract with a vendor. Instead of just haggling over price, think about what else you can bring to the table. Maybe you can offer them exposure to your audience or a longer commitment in exchange for a better rate. By shifting the focus from a zero-sum game to a collaborative effort, you both walk away feeling like winners.

Now, here's a little secret: empathy is your best friend in negotiations. Put yourself in their shoes. How would you feel if you were in their position? This perspective not only helps you understand their needs but also builds rapport. When they see you're genuinely interested in finding a solution that works for both sides, trust starts to blossom. And trust? Well, that's the foundation of any successful negotiation.

Another tactic to consider is the power of questions. Asking the right questions can open doors you didn't even know existed. Instead of making statements, turn it around. "What's important to you in this deal?" "How can we make this work for both of us?" These questions invite dialogue and create a space for collaboration. Plus, they give you valuable insights into what the other party truly values.

Now, let's not forget about preparation. It's like going into battle without armor if you don't do your homework. Research the other party. What's their history? What have they negotiated in the past? Knowing their patterns can give you an edge. And hey, don't underestimate the power of practice. Role-playing different scenarios with a friend can help you feel more confident when it's go-time.

As we wrap up this section, remember this: negotiation isn't just about getting your way. It's about creating a relationship that can flourish long after the deal is done. It's about finding common ground and building bridges. So, go out there, embrace the dance of negotiation, and remember that every conversation is an opportunity to learn and grow. You've got this!

Now, take a moment to visualize your next negotiation. Picture yourself sitting across from the other party, confidently presenting your ideas while actively listening to theirs. Feel that sense of purpose. You're not just negotiating; you're crafting a future where both sides can thrive.

So, what's next? Grab a pen and jot down your negotiation goals. What do you want to achieve? What are the interests behind those goals? And most importantly, how can you create win-win solutions? This is your journey, and you're well on your way to mastering the art of negotiation. Keep pushing forward, and remember—every step you take brings you closer to your success.

Chapter 14

Overcoming Objections

Objections—those annoying little bumps in the road that pop up when you're cruising along the persuasion highway. But listen up! They're not the end of the line; they're just speed bumps you can glide over with some savvy. Each objection? It's a hidden gem waiting to be discovered. So, let's roll up our sleeves and see how you can spot, reframe, and turn those objections into bridges that strengthen your influence.

First, let's tackle the art of anticipating objections. Imagine this: you're at a family get-together, chatting about your latest business idea. You can almost see the wheels turning in someone's head. "Is this really gonna fly? What if it tanks?" Classic, right? But here's the twist—if you can predict these objections before they pop up, you can prep your responses in advance.

Start by stepping into your audience's shoes. What are their fears? What concerns might they have about your proposal, product, or idea? Write 'em down. The more you get their perspective, the better you'll be at addressing those worries directly. It's like having a GPS for your journey—you know where the potholes are, so you can dodge 'em.

Now, here's where it gets juicy. When you anticipate objections, you can tackle them head-on. Don't wait for someone to bring it up.

Instead, beat them to the punch! "I know some folks might be wondering if this is worth their time or money, and that's totally valid." This not only shows you're in tune with their feelings but also builds trust. It's like saying, "Hey, I see you. I'm here for you."

Next, let's dive into reframing concerns. This is where the magic really kicks in. When someone raises an objection, it usually stems from fear or misunderstanding. Your mission? Gently shift their viewpoint. Think of it as flipping a frown upside down. Instead of seeing objections as roadblocks, treat them as chances to clarify and enlighten.

For example, if someone thinks your product's too pricey, don't just defend the cost. Reframe it! "I get that the upfront price might seem steep, but let's consider the long-term benefits. This investment will save you time and cash down the line." By reframing, you're not just addressing their worry; you're giving them a new lens to see the situation. It's like handing them a fresh pair of glasses to spot the value.

But here's the kicker—reframing isn't just about putting a positive spin on things. It's about being real and transparent. If there's a downside, own it! "Sure, it might take a bit to see results, but trust me, the wait will be worth it." This honesty builds trust, and trust? That's the bedrock of influence.

Now, let's shift gears and look at turning objections into chances for connection. This is where you really shine. When someone voices a concern, it's a golden opportunity to engage on a deeper level. Don't just brush off their objections—invite them to chat. Ask questions. "What specifically worries you about this?" This shows you value their input and are genuinely interested in finding a solution together.

By doing this, you're not just overcoming an objection; you're building a relationship. You're saying, "I care about your thoughts, and I want to work together to figure this out." This connection is powerful. It flips the script from adversarial to collaborative. You're not just a salesperson; you're a partner in their journey.

Let's pause for a real-world example. Picture yourself in a meeting, pitching a new marketing strategy. Halfway through, someone raises their hand and says, "I don't think this will resonate with our audience." Instead of getting defensive, you take a breath and say, "That's a solid point. Can you share what parts you think might miss the mark?" This opens up a dialogue, and suddenly, you're not just defending your idea; you're co-creating a solution that addresses their concerns while enhancing your proposal.

I get it—objections can feel like a punch in the gut. But here's the deal: every objection is a chance to sharpen your message, strengthen your relationship, and boost your influence. Embrace them!

As you keep moving forward, remember to practice these techniques. Role-play with a buddy or colleague. Anticipate objections in your daily chats. The more you practice, the more natural it'll feel. You'll start seeing objections not as barriers but as stepping stones to deeper connections and greater influence.

To wrap it up, overcoming objections isn't just a skill; it's an art. It's about listening, understanding, and connecting. It's about flipping doubt into dialogue and turning concerns into collaboration. So, next time you hit an objection, take a deep breath and remember: you've got this! Embrace the challenge, lean into the conversation, and watch your influence soar. Your journey's just getting started, and the world's ready for your unique voice. Keep pushing ahead, and let's make some magic happen!

Chapter 15

Measuring Influence and Success

Figuring out how you're doing isn't just about crunching numbers and staring at graphs. It's about feeling the vibe of your impact. You've worked hard, laid out your plans, and now it's time to see if they're hitting the mark. Think of it like a farmer watching over their crops. You don't just toss seeds in the ground and bounce. Nah, you're checking the weather, the soil, and how things are growing. So grab your metaphorical shovel, and let's dig in!

First things first, you gotta track how well your strategies are working. This is where the real magic happens. Sure, data might sound scary, but it's just info that tells you what's a hit and what's a miss. Start simple—maybe a journal or a spreadsheet, whatever floats your boat. Jot down your goals, what you did, and the results. Did folks engage? Did your sales spike? Did your message start buzzing?

Here's a pro tip: set specific, measurable goals. Instead of saying, "I want more people to read my blog," go for something like, "I want to boost my blog readership by 20% in the next three months." Now that's something you can track!

Next up, let's chat about feedback. Ah, feedback—the love-hate relationship of creativity. It can sting a bit, but it's also your best bud. Don't dodge it. Embrace it! Use feedback to sharpen your approach. Ask your audience what they think. You might be shocked by what they say. Maybe they dig your storytelling but want more practical tips. Or perhaps they enjoy your humor but get lost in the jargon. Whatever it is, listen up!

It's kinda like tuning a guitar. Sometimes you gotta tweak the strings to get that sweet sound. So take that feedback and adjust your strategies. It's all part of the ride. Remember, every piece of feedback is a stepping stone to getting better.

And let's not forget about celebrating your wins. Did you smash your readership goal? High-five! Did someone drop a glowing review? Time for confetti! Celebrating your successes—big or small—keeps your motivation alive. It reminds you why you kicked off this journey in the first place.

But hey, setbacks are part of the deal.
They're gonna happen, no doubt about it.
Maybe a campaign tanked, or a message didn't
land. Instead of sulking, flip the script. What
can you learn? What changes can you make
next time?

Think of setbacks as lessons dressed up in
disappointment. You're not just measuring
success; you're measuring growth. Each
stumble teaches you something new, and that's
pure gold in the influence game.

So as you move forward, keep this in mind:
track your strategies, soak up feedback, and
celebrate your journey. Your influence is a
living thing, and by measuring it, you're not just
checking success—you're building a legacy.

Take a sec to visualize your success. Picture
your audience, all engaged and transformed by

what you're sharing. Feel the energy of your influence ripple through them. That's the power you've got!

Now, let's break it down into some easy steps.

1. Set specific, measurable goals for your strategies.

2. Keep a journal or spreadsheet to track your actions and outcomes.

3. Actively seek feedback from your audience and use it to refine your approach.

4. Celebrate your wins, no matter how small they seem.

5. Analyze setbacks and pull out valuable lessons for future growth.

You've got this! Each step gets you closer to
mastering the art of influence. Remember, it's
not just about the endgame; it's about the
journey and the lives you're touching along the
way. So keep your chin up, your heart open, and
let your influence shine bright!

Index